imagination series # 3

HAMMERLOCK

Poems by Tim Seibles

Cleveland State University Poetry Center

ACKNOWLEDGEMENTS

Many thanks to the following journals where some of these poems first appeared: *Artful Dodge, Callaloo, Calliope, Controlled Burn, Crab Orchard Review, Hanging Loose, Kenyon Review, New Letters, New Texas, Ploughshares, The Progressive, Red Brick Review, Tex!,* and *The Texas Observer.*

"Manic: A Conversation with Jimi Hendrix" appeared in the anthology *Outsiders*, Milkweed Press, 1999

"Marrow" and "Valentine's Day" appeared in the anthology *Dark Eros*, St. Martin's Press, 1997.

"Commercial Break: Road-Road Runner, Uneasy," "Kerosene," and "What You Really Want" appeared in the anthology *Leaning House Poetry, Volume I*, Leaning House Press, 1996.

"Latin" appeared in the anthology *A Way Out of No Way*, Henry Holt, 1996.

I would like to thank Martha Christina of Ampersand Press for her work on the chapbook, *Kerosene*, in which several of these poems first appeared.

Thanks also to Robert Wynne of Mille Grazie Press for his work on the chapbook, *Ten Miles An Hour*, which featured several works found in this collection.

Special thanks to the Provincetown Fine Arts Works Center for a fellowship that made much of this work possible.

Special thanks also to Renée Olander for all of her help and encouragement.

Published by Cleveland State University Poetry Center
1983 East 24th Street
Cleveland, OH 44115-2440

ISBN 1-880834-45-6

Library of Congress Catalog
Card Number: 99-72725

The Ohio Arts Council helped fund this program with state tax dollars to encourage economic growth, educational excellence and cultural enrichment for all Ohioans.

CONTENTS

I

II

III

IV

for my parents,
Thomas & Barbara Seibles

and for my fellow artists
who just keep keepin' on

I

CHECK OUTSIDE

They believe that if they remain
frightened enough for long enough
things won't happen. You know— *things*.

Listen to a city late at night:
the dead-bolts clapped into place,
tv's spitting on the floor, upstairs
mothers hammering Jesus
into their black thumbs.

But things will happen. Even here
with everybody here. People are going
to do some more things. You see it
all the time. Starting now

and from now on, weather is weather,
and news is weather too.
Who do you think is behind
all those uniforms? Your plans:

your ideas   about tomorrow.
Even now, the blood turns
in your ear— a story. You want
a story.

But right now we're right
in the middle of something really
funny, and let me tell you: it's something
like a story, all this.

People with chips— heavy chips
on their shoulders. People with a few
tricks up their sleeves   have
got to do some more.   things.

Check outside— how the wind runs
from some exact somewhere. That man
near the wall by the *7-11*. What's
he got in his hand?

WHAT BUGS BUNNY SAID
TO RED RIDING HOOD

Say, good lookin, what brings you out thisaway
amongst the fanged and the fluffy?
Grandma, huh?
Some ol bag too lazy to pick up a pot, too feeble
to flip a flapjack—
and you all dolled up like a fire engine
to cruise these woods?

This was your **mother's** idea?
She been livin in a *CrackerJack* box or somethin?
This is a tough neighborhood, mutton chops—
you gotchur badgers, your wild boar, your
hardcore grizzlies   and lately,
this one wolf's been actin pretty big and bad.

I mean, what's up, doc?
Didn anybody ever tell you it ain't smart
to stick out in wild places?
Friendly? You want friendly you better
try Detroit. I mean
you're safe wit me, sweetcakes,
but I ain't a meat-eater.

You heard about Goldie Locks, didn'cha? Well,
didn'cha? Yeah, well, little Miss Sunshine—
little Miss *I'm-so-much-cuter-than-thee*—
got caught on one of her sneaky porridge runs
and the Three Bears weren't in the mood:
so last week the game warden nabs baby bear
passin out her fingers to his pals.

That's right. Maybe your motha should
turn off her soaps, take a peek at a newspaper,
turn on some cartoons, for Pete's sake:
this woyld is about teeth, bubble buns— who's bitin
and who's getting bit. The noyve a'that broad
sendin you out here lookin like a ripe tomata.
Why don't she just hang a sign aroun your neck:
Get over here and bite my legs off!
Cover me wit mustid—   call me a hotdawg!

Alright, alright, I'll stop.
Listen, Red, I'd hate for somethin upleasant
to find you out here all alone.
Grandma-shmandma— let'er call *Domino's.*
They're paid to deliver. Besides, toots,
it's already later than you think—
get a load a'that chubby moon up there.

Ya can't count on Casper tanight either.
They ran that potata-head outta town two months ago—
tryin ta make friends all the time—
he makes you sick after awhile.

Look, Cinderella, I got some candles and some
cold uncola back at my place— whaddaya say?

Got any artichokies in that basket?

HARDIE

You know how tiny kids walk up to you, raise their arms
and expect to be picked up— I used to do that; that was me.

Me, with my diaper full and my nose half-crusty.

I remember being eye to eye with the little doors
underneath the kitchen sink— I was a child, seriously.

I used to yank open those cabinets and see the shiny colors
and glass: the orange box of Tide, the pink bottle leaking
dishwashing liquid, a green Pine Sol thing with big yellow letters.

Of course, I couldn't read and before I could touch anything
my mom was snatching me back, slapping my hands—

that shit hurt! My hands were really little, really
new, like shoots fresh out of the ground,
really soft— I was a child. Is that clear?

People just put me to bed whenever they felt like it.
People sat me on the potty every other whenever
and said *Go!*

I didn't have any words, just sloppy, muddy kinds of garbled
clucks
that wanted to be words, that tried to be wordish—

think of the amount of criticism I got. Criticism piled on
like cold cream of wheat.

It was like I couldn't do anything right— not a goddamn thing!

Picture *me* in a high chair being pressured to eat.
They might have been dangling a secret agent off a cliff
trying to make him give up something top-secret.

I was little; my legs hardly held me up; everybody
stood around poised to catch me—

Ooops!   Oooopsy!   Whoops-a-daisy!

How could I get my confidence?

But now I'm big, I eat ice cream all the time— I'm big; I use
the *Men's* room; nobody tells me what to do,

even though I feel like I'm holding onto my life the way a
wounded ant clings to a window screen. I'm

big now. Big and musty. Big enough to hide my baby shoes
in the palm of one hand.

But once I was a kid. I didn't
need deodorants. I sat on my grandmother's lap
and ate candy spearmint leaves.

I wasn't down on white people. I
didn't even know I was black. My whole bag
was cartoons— I was a child, goddammit!

Just a mouthful of Tonka Toys and Lego,
a little guy with no sense of time passing.
Where was everybody going? What happened to *Johnny Quest*?!

Next thing I know, I got this *hardie* thumping around
on my belly— every morning, fearless,
like my own bad-ass rooster— sun-up and *cock-a-
doodle-doo!*

I couldn't pee with it and nobody would tell me
what it was for.

I wasn't always so worldly. I wasn't always a madman
over women's legs either. I spent my first fifteen years
without a real kiss.

I was a child. You think I don't remember?!
You think it's easy keeping all this innocence pent up inside?!

And now, when it comes to money, I'm like some dizzy insect
full of wanting it, like some big bluebottle fly
tipsy over a mound of shit.

I wasn't always like this.

Parts of me started getting large, growing hair:
my underarms, my wrists, even the tops of my feet.

But I *was* a little boy once: really curious, really small.
really scared—

Is that clear?

THE CAPS ON BACKWARD

It was already late inside me.

City air. City light.
Houses in a row.

14-year-olds. Nine of us.
Boys.

Eight voices changed. Already rumbling
under the governance of sperm.

But *his* voice, bright as a kitten's
tickled our ears like a piccolo.

So, we'd trill ours up— *What's wrong, man?*
Cat got your balls?" And watch him shrink
like a dick in a cool shower.

Every day. Bit by bit. Smaller.

I think about it now— how bad he wanted to be
with us   how, alone with the radio

he must have worked his throat
to deepen the sound.

The blunt edge of boys   teething on each other.
The serrated edge of things in general.

Maybe he spilled grape soda on my white sneaks.

Can't remember.

But I knocked him down, gashed him with my fists.

It was summer. A schoolyard afternoon.
Older boys by the fountain.

Yeah, kick his pussy ass.

Nobody said it, but it was time.
We knew it   the way trees know shade
doesn't belong to them.

The low voices knew.
And the caps on backward.

It must go something like this:

First, one cell flares in the brain. Then
the two cells next to that. Then more and more.

Until something far off begins to flicker.
Manhood, the last fire lit before the blackening woods.

The weak one separated from the pack.

The painted bird. The bird, painted.

FROM THE DIARY OF
QUAI CHANG CAINE, SHAOLIN MONK

found in 1883
near McGehee, TX

My life, explained to flies, would have them laughing.

Two years ago I killed the Emperor's oldest son.

On the holy road to this Temple of Heaven
I buried a spear in his back
because one of the Royal Guard shot my old teacher, Po.

He had stumbled in front of the Prince's caravan.

A good man lost because those with power
have no time for those without it.

And it must be a strange pleasure   believing the world
was made only for you, that your wealth is proof,
that the breeze actually prefers your face.

I thought I would die in China that day—

with the large bounty offered by the Royal House
and the random hangings—

but the people kept my shadow in their pockets.

I have the robes that say I know
killing does no one honor,
that no injury is ever rightly avenged.

But what do I do with the ache in my blood
that was eased when I threw the spear?

February 1881 aboard
cargo ship "Yun Hee"

———————

Now, I am in Mescalero, New Mexico— America—
      a half-white Shaolin,
always only a few steps ahead of the price for my death.

Mostly, people here are hard-working and stupid.
If an American has two thoughts the first and the second
involve money.

Though skin lies simply along the surface of a man
people here think it is a sign of something deep— grace
if you are white   fault if you are not.

There are places where I can not get a glass of water.

By my eyes, they know I am not white, but by my height and color
they suspect that I am not *not* white.

October 1881
Carrizozo, NM

———————

Yesterday, I blinded someone
for spitting on my food. He laughed.
Then I reached into his face. It happened
so quickly— I swear, for that second,
my hand belonged to someone else.

———————

I have seen black people and red also and others not seen in China.

To witness hate coming to live along the lines of skin—
suppose some rabid animal were roaming the countryside,
everyone would agree to kill it, to stop it somehow. Here,
it is as if the people would take this thing in and feed it,
so quick they are to nurse this cruelty.

January 1882
Kenna, NM

———————————

It is unfortunate that the whites here are so many.
They have grown invisible to themselves   like the air
which is also everywhere.

In a hundred years
much will be regretted and very little forgiven.

May 1882
Paducah, TX

———————————

There is a woman named Qi Do.
Two eyes are not enough to hold the shimmer in her hair.
Some days I catch my heart trying to memorize her face.

A man, the sheriff's friend, tried to open her blouse.
I merely turned his hand and told him she was not
from the saloon.

He said he would peel me "like a slant-eyed banana."

When I killed the Prince, I became sick in my stomach,
though the Royal House is yet famous for torture.

When I killed the first assassin sent after me, it was like
slapping a mosquito poised to suck from my wrist.

Laotzu has written, *One who recognizes all men
as members of his own body
is a sound man to guard them.*

I am a priest. I believe in living
toward this. But often my anger occurs to me

as its own creature   with its own teeth.

July 1882
Knox City, TX

———————

To those who would sleep through the wounds
they inflict on others,
I offer pain to help them awaken, sometimes death to
keep them calm.

There is no question injustice can ask
to which violence is not a fair answer.

The man who wanted to peel me— I helped him
fit half his blade into his thigh,
his right hand still on the hilt.

The look on his face then:

as if he had seen a sparrow swallowing a wolf.

———————

All my life I have stood apart from other Chinese
because I looked white, and here   been outcast by whites
for the shape of my eyes. Now, I see beauty
in the motions of revenge, the making of harm—

so now   I am not even Shaolin.

But why should *belonging* be such a prize?
Except to one who needs others
to tell him his name.

Membership is only another word for obedience.
Obedience is for dogs and children.

I know who I am   but where can I

March 1883
Abilene, TX

Note: The Shaolin were a sect of Taoist priests in China, who were deeply
committed to peace. They were especially drawn to nature as a model of the
intrinsic harmony of living things. Much of their meditation was realized through
the practice of kung fu.

ON BEING MISTAKEN

I guess you could say
I am not who I am. I always
suspected there was
something about me.
The other day a brother cold stopped me,
"Man, I thought you was Rod from Pakistan!"

No wonder I'm suspicious
when somebody loves me.
How can they be sure that I'm not
who I am? Hell, I was happy the guy
had wanted to stop me.
I was feeling like Rod from Pakistan.

I think I've become who I
cannot become, so that is what I am.
In the Home of the Brave
plodding through my heart darkly,
I see things in *the dream* I just
can't understand.

At times I check mirrors,
and my gestures aren't like me—
a bashful half-smile and a
twitch in one hand.
In some ways I sense that my brain is
held hostage. I'm supposed to be
Rod from Pakistan.

People say, "Damn, you just let
your phone ring." It's because they keep calling

who they hope that I am.
If they knew me they'd know
most of this is for show— my real life
hasn't even really began.

I have to admit I don't know
where I am. I just wish I had known
I was not in the plans. Then you could say
It's not us— we're the same—
that *brother just ain't who* **he** *am.*
I'd be smooth as a tulip   absolute
and yours nearly,

                    sweet Rod
                        from Pakistan

COMMERCIAL BREAK: ROAD-RUNNER, UNEASY

If I didn't know better I'd say
the sun never moved ever,

that somebody just pasted it there
and said the hell with it,

but that's impossible.
After awhile you have to give up

those conspiracy theories.
I get the big picture. I mean,

how big can the picture be?
I actually think it's kind of funny—

that damn coyote always scheming,
always licking his skinny chops

and me, pure speed, the object of all
his hunger, the *everything* he needs—

talk about **impossible**, talk about
the grass is always greener . . .

I **am** the other side of the fence.

You've got to wonder, at least a little,
if this could be a set-up:

with all the running I do—
the desert, the canyons, the hillsides, the desert—

all this open road   has got to
lead somewhere   else. I mean,

that's what freedom's all about, right?
Ending up where you want to be.

I used to think it was funny— *Road-runner*
the coyote's after you   Road-runner . . .

Now, I'm mainly tired. Not that
you'd ever know. I mean,

I can still make the horizon
in two shakes of a snake's tongue,

but it never gets easier out here, alone
with Mr. Big Teeth and his ACME supplies:

leg muscle vitamins, tiger traps,
instant tornado seeds.

C'mon! I'm no tiger.
And who's making all this stuff?

I can't help being a little uneasy.
I do one of my tricks,

a rock-scorching, razor turn at 600 miles an hour,
and he falls off the cliff, the coyote—

he really falls: I see the small explosion
his body slamming into dry dirt

so far down in the canyon
the river looks like a crayon doodle.

That has to hurt, right?
Five seconds later, he's just up the highway

hoisting a huge anvil
above a little, yellow dish of bird feed—

like I don't see what's goin' on. C'mon!

You know how sometimes, even though you're
very serious about the things you do,

it seems like, secretly, there's a
big joke being played,

and you're part of what
someone else is laughing at— only

you can't prove it, so you
keep sweating and believing in

your *career*, as if that
makes the difference, as if somehow

playing along   isn't really

playing along as long as you're
not sure what sort of fool

you're being turned into, especially
if you're giving it *100%*.

So, when I see dynamite
tucked under the ACME road-runner cupcakes,

as long as I don't wonder why my safety
isn't coming first in this situation,

as long as I don't think me
and the coyote are actually

working for the same people,

as long as I eat and

get away   I'm not really stupid,

right? I'm just fast.

WHAT THE WIND SAYS

after David Swanger

The wind says, "I am the past beside you, a scratch
on your lens, lips that opened easily and wetly

took you in. You might lose the map, but the road
I poured to your heart will still shimmer. I am

neither air brewing, nor either hand set afire, not God
strumming the Earth, nor jeweled anger in rottweiler eyes.

You think you are someone to be reckoned with, a star
pinned above your crotch, your best day
tucked inside your vest like the ace of spades. You

believe what you read is trying to mean something
in some acceptable way. Pitiful. Take your thumb
out of your mouth. Mainly what you miss

matters most— which is why I am the saliva
lost on your neck from a kiss, the slash
in the air where you sit, long fingers pushed
inside you, the shoe words cobble while you sleep.

I know you want to run into trouble, to make news
as some chalk figure on the street. I know
you've almost broken through to the present,
only to turn back to a pimple in your mirror.

Since you have fumbled at love, you believe we
all sigh with you, that when you end up
on the wet spot I know the chill and sympathize.

Forget that shit! Imagine, this moment,
all your organs humming together like a choir
of roots in damp earth. Could everything

be wrapped up in *your* destination? Think.
Think of how early becomes evening, how blind fish
find each other from opposite sides of the dark.
Think how sexy I am, because of what I keep from you."

NEVER DAYTIME

People don't like to think about their organs, about

what's happening exactly inside the old abdominal walls.

I mean, it's never daytime in there.

The germs, the sly toxins   getting together, moving around

Think about it: the heart preening and flexing itself
always in the pitch black.

And your blood never knows how candy-apple red it is
until you hurt yourself. Too late then.

And the big, scary lungs   sucking on the big, invisible air,

pulling it down into the basement, roughing it up,
then shoving it back upstairs.

No one wants to imagine what's going on— really—
with their vitals, which one is feeling

just a little bit down in the mouth   Or maybe a tad cancerous
or a little like just calling it quits: the liver? the kidneys?

some clogged tubal something in the reproductive stuff?

Once you're born, look at all the trouble you can have.

Sometimes there are shows on television
that show what it looks like in there.

Some tiny camera poking around   or the body sliced open
for a team of surgeons   like a ripe melon at a party.

And it's all gooey and nasty-lookin and squishy.

Your giblets. On parade.

Your organs, like a club of deviants, found
rubbing up against each other with the lights off.

There's never any real supervision.

It's easier not thinking about it— of course, it is.

Suppose you had dear, dear relatives living in a town where
it was midnight all the time— and say you knew
criminals wandered the streets with the switchblades, with
nothing better to do—

The things that could happen. The bad chances swarming
like a ticked-off buncha' bees.

At first, you would worry all the time, every minute: *Poor Drusilla! Hold on, Uncle Chuck!* You couldn't sleep. You wouldn't taste your food.

Then, you'd have to kinda forget about them. It'd just be too much.

What about your gizzards right now, keeping you in the game—
but why   why should they? What kind of life do they have?

The intestines. You got a set workin 24/7   holding, handling, moving
what you don't even want a whiff of. And it goes on and on.

Sorry. No gloves or aerosols or vacations for the chitlins.

Better not think about it.
Better think about stuff you can fold up or dry-clean.

Otherwise, your mind'll get all out of control.

THE APPLECAKE

for Hermann Michaeli

On days like this,
on Tuesdays— when sad buffalo
moo blues inside me, and what sun there is
fizzles above my crooked hat
like a dud fuse, on Wednesdays
when a man wears his solitude
like an iron yoke, when a woman strings
her necklace with the same rage
that split the moon,
when itchy children lean
against windows waiting while rain
whips the sidewalks.

When all over the everywhere trouble
chain smokes and spits, and
people wonder why they
don't have no money, why the priests
are tipsy with sin, why the police
have turned against them,
on Thursdays
when pigeons start barking
and the rats have
already nibbled God down
to a hairy nose, when every president
is Reagan, when it all seems lost
and wrong and too far for any
luck to reach,

I like to consider your applecake
smiling on the kitchen counter, dressed
only in its sweetness, its round face
a jubilant island of apple and sugar—
no mere strudel or sloppy cobbler—
it is a baked cathedral of promises
kept, your applecake
opening up like a three-day weekend,
a Good Friday for one's mouth, a jailbreak
from the hard, inedible, unthinkable city.

How do you do it, my friend?
What is the recipe? More than teaspoons
and cups, food words and measures,
the magic must hide in your hands
like invisible fruit—
each finger become secretly
a buttery bough of apples blazing slowly,
each year of your life changed
to flavor, each memory— even the ones
that bruise the soul— a nameless spice,
a lamp intended to go on, to glow
in the hope-laden tongue of the world.

The applecake, like a circular avenue
around and around which the friendliest
lovers move— in no hurry
to be anyplace but your arms forever,

for an afternoon— the applecake,
like a sacred lens through which
the real earth might be seen— a blue ruby
pinned to a golden scarf
of near, near stars— the delicious earth
done with barracuda greed
and bone-headed hate,

the applecake itself   a new planet
where everything plays everything and all
is always well— big towns full
of pals, mambo music, polkas, hip-
hop, the very air drunk
with cooking— where someone lonely,

someone sincerely complicated,
can put his arms around
a warm slice, or wrestle a big piece
to the floor, and without
saying anything, with only a parting
of his lips,
make a perfect night of it.

II

THE HERD

Some of the light, some of the first light
arrived so softly it could have been dew
drawn from the night air, and in the creamy-
blue distance thunderheads flickered.

They were still sleeping then, scattered
under trees or in groups in the open,
their slate-colored flanks lightening.

Overnight three had been killed, but the wild dogs
were gone now and the scavengers too,
and the lake began to show dawn its muddy edges.

What was surprising was that they ever slept
at all— with so many things alive in the dark,
but they slept well, dreaming exactly what they
dreamed they should dream, and when the strongest one
rolled back the silence with a long, throbbing yawn,

the others answered, divvying up the air
with staccato croaks, shrill bleats and near-
growls— some with front legs still bent
under them, some with eyes caught shining
as if they had never before seen the world.

No one knew how long they had been here
or what to call them   Or how it was that they came
to understand themselves, what to do, where to go.

But they moved together like a slow wind,
as a wind moves from one place to another,
dying off but rising again, the same wind moving.

And when the must broke into their blood
they coupled fiercely, almost in a panic, as if
one by one they were beginning to drown— the heat
sliding over each in turn like the shadow of a cloud.

––––––––––––––

Once it had cleared the treetops, the sun paved
the veldt bright yellow, and the stilt-legged birds
that had been chitter-whistling since early early,
quieted; some stood in the shallows
stabbing the lake for lazy, flat-headed fish.

The herd was eating too, nudging each other for room,
nostrils flexing wet and open. You might have
thought they'd been made for nothing but
filling their mouths, so content did they seem
tugging at the stringy greens with their square teeth.

They were not stupid; though sometimes when weather
changed unexpectedly, they would simply stampede
barrel-eyed while the rain snapped against their backs.
And if one among them bore some odd marking,
when it reached a certain age, the others
drove it away with head-butts and hard kicks.

I saw it happen once: a female with a bronze-colored face
instead of the usual gray, limped a short ways
behind the herd, her right foreleg fractured.
Each time she tried to rejoin they attacked— mainly
the bulls and ranking cows— stomping, frothing,
fussing up immense heaves of dust.

The wounded animal seemed confused, not seeing, not
being able to see what was wrong, unable to keep

from following, just as the attackers couldn't
stop themselves, couldn't understand what stranged
inside their skulls to turn them against their own.

———————————

The dogs were made for this—
their sharp, felt-furred ears barely visible,
gliding above the high weeds by the lake,
and when they took the open field their feet
kissed the earth for allowing such speed
and the taste of meat and they were upon her
and the air turned over, so heavy with the smell
of blood, it was nearly animal itself.

Hard to say what went on inside the herd
with death blossoming right there,
or if any had actually watched the kill,
or if it made a difference either way.
The dogs would always be there
blind but for their teeth, and the herd
would continue to find the sunrise
next to the dark, returning from sleep
to offer their young to the flat world.

And was it anything like sorrow
that brought a few back days later
to scuff the ground where that one
with the new face had fallen?

Or just some dumb itch of memory,
some lizard's blink of deja-vu,
the future circling
to take them along.

THE CASE

White people don't know they're   white.

Newspaper.   Coffee.   Gosh-whataday!

Not everyone doesn't admire them. In fact,
a lot of people like their *time-for-the-news* TV voices.

It's not that they're not beautiful. Just check out a beach.
Oh, they're beautiful all right.

Sometimes though, if you're not white
and a lot of other people are—
but they don't know it:

Well, it can make you feel like you need to be somewhere
way far away.

And if you go to the supermarket and look
at the magazine racks   you might start getting
that "uh-oh" feeling.

Most of the time you just laugh, that's all— you just
have to laugh   and probably shake lots of hands.

Once a woman I worked with said
I never even **think** *of you as black.*

She was being un- pre- ju- diced.

You shouldn't get angry about stuff though.

I know some brothers, they see a white face
and their whole bodies sneer—

even if everything was going perfect that day, even
if the white face never did anything,
never said nothin'.

And then, of course, there are the Nazi-like skinheads
and the other etceteras

who wannabe all about whiteness— hating the gooks,
the spics, and all the geronimos et cetera.

Oh, they're white enough all right.

THE STUPID

I no longer know what it means.
I no longer know what to say about
anything that has anything
to do with anything— not that
anyone else has ever really known ever
before either, but I hold the record
for consecutive days totally dumbfounded.
Watch this: See what I mean?
It's in my eyes— I am ignorant
of everything to a very large degree,
to a degree so large in fact that
if this degree were a fly-swatter
you could smash all of Philadelphia with it,
or if this degree were a planet it'd be
Jupiter. See what I mean? Nobody should even
talk to me, not even a nervous hello
from someone white passing me on the street,
not even a sidelong growl from some
mange-ravaged mutt named Mortimer,
not with all this stupid I've got piled up
inside. I'm so stupid I'm not even sure
I'm stupid. I no longer know
what it means— know what I mean?
I wake up all excited and can't remember
what was what in my dreams. I let
somebody take my pulse and now
I need the damn thing— to locate my
wrists, just to find my hands. Last week
I picked up an encyclopedia, you know,

trying to find a cure, and the sucker
shriveled up like a cold prune's penis.
That's what a bad case of stupid can do.
Somebody starts a war— next thing you know
you're tying yellow ribbons on everything.
Once, after the riot, I saw the President
sound-biting about what caused the thing
in L.A., about how it had nothing to do
with race, and I knew, for certain, the stupid
had made a mess of him. Now it's me—
one telethon won't do it, not ten probably
either, but research is a start I guess.
I just wish I knew where I caught it.
Ask me anything about America: See what I mean?

BILLY JACK, SERVING 25 TO LIFE

for Tom Laughlin

Well, I'm not sure how I did it,
but for a minute there was a brushfire
in my blood— like my body finally understood
exactly what rage was for, and before
I knew it, the tall guy was down on his knees
spittin out teeth, and the mouthy dude
with the wide-brim was movin towards me.
Sometimes there's nothing else to do
but hit somebody with all your might,
and really, it's something like kissing someone
you've had a crush on for years—
it's so perfect that first moment
of contact; there's such a hunger in it:
driving the nose bone into the brain,
the soul, in all its loneliness, finally
married to a single, well-aimed fist.

Growing up, I never knew how much I'd love
the sunset for coming without tricks,
the way a day closes with the light
giving up after trying so hard
to keep everything clear. When I looked
into my father's dark Seminole face,
I didn't think I'd ever know why
he gripped a bottle like a torch
or what he meant when he'd say, "Billy,
your mother's people— goddamn! They
make you wanna rip the horns
offa chargin bull!" Now
I guess I do.

But I don't resent my mother's white skin.
When she twined her blood with his,
she became something different   as I
am different from both of them. I knew
white people didn't like us, but it
wasn't till those two men from Texas
broke Eduardo's legs and poured flour
on his face that it started to reach me.
We were 15, and they had that iron pipe—
all I could do was run— and whenever
I think about it, even after 22 years,
it's like finding a gash in my chest.

There's nothing wrong with being white,
unless you think that   that complexion
means everyone darker than you is here
for your entertainment. This sickness
has been so well armed and so well
organized for so long, and people
seem so willing to be stupid: white
supremacists   or friendly bigots
who like Michael Jordan
on their *Wheaties* box, people who
believe in Columbus, who don't see
anything *all that bad* about naming a team
the "Redskins." And after awhile you get
tired of explaining patiently, setting
the **good example**, ignoring the little jokes,
trying to squeeze a drop of brotherhood
out of a pile of dumb-ass rocks. You get
tired– know what I mean?
You just get fed the hell up.

So, nine months and four days ago
I was in this place 3 hours west of here
with Silk Water Su, a black Cherokee
who tells me she gets her name from the creek
behind her house, but I say it's the way
her body washes over you when she
wants it to, the way her body shines, kinda
shimmers like a river lit late in the day.
Anyway, it *was* evening and the sun
had just about set and we were walkin slow
lookin in store windows when some guy
half-shadowed in a doorway said, "Look,
some nigger and a redskin— in *our* town—
sniffin for scraps." Well,

I stopped and stood there for
I don't know how long,
not sayin shit   just thinkin,
even though Su told me to *let it slide*.
I thought about those two words
and all the bad history squeezed
inside them: slave ships, the Ghost
Dance, lynch mobs, land stole,
children starved, smallpox, backs
beat bloody over cotton, Sand Creek,
and all the white books
full of applause.

I thought about how many decent,
hard-working, reasonable human beings

have been *redskinned* and *niggered* and *spicked*
into whiskey-swiggin, dope-suckin, dull-eyed,
pigeon-hearted people— all because some
snow-faced, cross-carryin crackers couldn't
quite get done stompin on their throats.

And I thought about Silk Water with her
smiling high-dimpled, brown cheeks, trying
to stay calm in her steady push toward some
goddamned idea of nobody's-ever-seen-it
justice— how she winces   then lets it go
whenever these sad, sorry-ass motherfuckers
rise up happy to spit in her beautiful face.
And I tried, I   really   did   try
to stay cool, to roll with it, to turn
that other cheek   they keep talkin about,
but I only have one heart   and so many of us
have had to "Yassir" and "Si Señor" and grin
"Heap-big-Indian" grins for people who just
balled up our lives and watched us bleed,

that when he said nigger again
stepping out into the soft orange light
with three of his friends, I just   I
guess I just, well, it was like
the sun suddenly turned around and
rose again, and I could see
the tall guy's teeth clearly, clenched
in this clean-cut, good-time smile— really,
he was smiling.

NOT ANYMORE

for Mary Behrens

People don't know they're animals.

People go around worrying and brushing their teeth.

But we're stuffed to the gills with instincts.

Germs climb onto us, get into our mouths.
They have a field day.

And dogs know what's under our clothes—

balls   vaginas.
They have some too.

       Hunt.

People know they're animals.
Everybody does what everybody else does in the bathroom.
People realize it's got to   come out.

Men don't like being animals.   Women really don't like it.

Then come the urges.

Uh-oh.

And we actually have sperms and eggs and menstrual stuff—
animal goo of all kinds.

Language.

My parents are not animals.   Not anymore.

Dad reads *National Geographic*.
Mom jazzercises with Richard Simmons.

Sometimes I feel myself salivating.

And you can say what you want, but there is movement
inside me   like some restless, edgy four-legger
pacing.   My blood   thinking.

The way animals must think   through some set of inner shoves.

Like hunger, the belly nudging the brain
to go get some chips, get an apple.

The way being horny turns you toward the telephone.

Human.

Listen to a stadium some Sunday afternoon.

Watch the pack keeping on its shoes.

Those drumsticks, all those cheeseburgers—
some animals were using those chunks of muscle
to carry themselves around.

THIS IS THE REASON

Some people were playing cards . . . and among the players
was a young man who at one point, without saying
anything, laid down his cards, left the bar, ran across the
deck, and threw himself into the sea. By the time the boat
was stopped   . . . the body couldn't be found.

– Marguerite Duras
from *The Lover*

This. This white railing. This
something like sorrow,

something like a scraped knee—
but in your brain. This long wait

with whatever's next
like powdered glass on your tongue. This.

These hands. These dead stars
shuffling the dark. This ache like ice

on a tooth, only
all the time, like a time you

really needed to say something. This
itching scab in the heart.

This something
like not breathing when

you're breathing. This. This
Pepsi jingle, the newspaper,

these insects, this evening, that cigarette.

HANK THE GULL

What part'a this is hard for you?
When a bird flies, he flies— he ain't
showin' off. He's got a job.
You don't see me 'n' the flock
all fluffed up. Forgetaboutit!
I'm tellin' you— when a bird flies,
he's just wingin' it. It's like
walkin'   except in the air.

People always say, "Oh, I wish
I could fly. It's so graceful, so
free!" Look, you hairy heads,
you got stuff to do— *we* got stuff to do.
Responsabilidies!

You and your bags'a crumbs.
You guys see a coupl'a Canada V's
and you think it's always a vacation,
like everything's a cruise.
I got your vacation— *right here!*
Cruise on *this*.

I mean what's the big deal?
A bird flies, he flies. Awright-awready,
I guess it's a little beautiful, but
people walk around, you don't see us
fallin' outta the sky. Your knees bend,
your feet sort'a glide— looks beautiful.
The point is ya get where ya gotta go.

Wings is like feet wit' feathers.
Arms is like wings wit'out feathers.
When I get the lift, I'm not flittin' aroun'
looky, looky— I'm airborne!
Okay, maybe the first time, but hey,
now the wind's in my beak. I got errands.
Jus' like you eggbeaters witchur
greazy little *fingers* all over everything.

When a bird flies, he flies.
Forgetaboutit! He takes off.
But he's gotta come back. So
what's so frickin' free? You got feet—
I don't see no fence aroun' you—
you free?
Yeah, pal, I got your freedom . . .

ABOUT FREEDOM

We want you to be yourself.
We want you to feel free to express yourself— as you are.
We do.

You **should** be yourself.
After all, who else can you be?
Not her. Not him. Not those guys with the hats.

Be the real you— anything else will be phony.

But be nice.
Play by the rules. Think of the rules
when you play. The rules are there for everybody.
So nobody gets hurt.

Everybody plays. Everybody benefits.
Nobody wants any trouble.

And every single one of us should be him and her self
while playing.
Each person, a unique presence in the world, free to be
whoever he or she was born to be.

Each a seed, a seedling, growing its own way to the sun.

Of course, what other way could you grow— but your own?
Can't expect a baby chick to become a crocodile.
An acorn is meant to be an oak tree.

That's just the way it is.
Who can blame anybody for growing into the thing
she was meant to be?

You got talent? You gotta use it to do something
about what you see.

Nobody's gonna tell anybody not to feel what he feels.

It'd be like **me** blaming **you** for being what you are.
It'd be like **me** blaming **you** for not being *me*.

That's what the rules are there for— so things keep making sense.
So while we're growing we'll know what we're doing.
Can't grow in the dark.

You ever see plants   try to grow in the dark?
Some light is helpful. Rules are a kind of light.

You've been lost before without a map.
Feels bad. Rules are a kind of map.
Without them you could end up just anywhere—

Suppose everybody ended up all over the place.
It'd be weird.   There'd be chaos.   It'd be scary.

People would do things with no thought of the consequences.

Consequences make the world go round.

If Rules are the Bride   Consequences are the Groom.

Consequences keep everybody   playing   by the *rules*.
See, if you don't play by the rules there are consequences.
And you don't want those.

Consequences are what you get when you do things
that **aren't** on the map.
Consequences are meant to make you wish you
didn't have to face them.

But you will face them.
Because that's what consequences are for.

For people like you. Who don't understand exactly
what it means

to go too far. Consequences are there to show you exactly
where *too far* is— and why you shouldn't go there,

to teach you the way a razor teaches a finger
not to slide along the edge.
To teach you something you won't soon forget

about freedom
and the things you might want to do with it—

and what's so bad about that?

OUTTAKES FROM AN INTERVIEW
WITH MALCOLM X AFTER MECCA

January 1965

My going to prison simply made it clear
that I had already been in prison.
If you misinform a man his mind becomes a cage,
and everything he does is just him
reaching a paw between the bars; you get too close,
you get clawed. Next question.

Now, I think you already know what television
means to me: Cowboys   Indians   Bo-Jangles dancing
with that little blond girl   *Tarzan*   and that
damn collie, *Lassie*— white people picture themselves
over and over as the good guys, but look what they've done.

You don't want me to lie, do you? When brown eyes
look into blue eyes— in this country—   how
can we not   get shoved up against these last 500 years?

No, America has not been anything like a melting pot
where black people are concerned, but it will be heating up— shortly.

Wait. Wait a minute. I **am** absolutely against people mistreating people.
It does not matter who   But if you've hurt somebody
for no reason   You've got to expect to get hurt
for *no reason*.   That's not radical.   That's human.
But these white folks, these *Christians*   killing and praying
for nothing but profit and some sick dream
of supremacy   and, on top of that, always assuming
the moral high ground— now **that's** radical.
You might even call that   *extreme.*

52

But you know I'm not writing the history books.
I'm too busy being dangerous   according to the news.
Even though no one has ever seen me hurt anybody.

And the papers can't get finished with all this about
"Hate Monger X" and "X advocates violent revolution."

Let me tell you, don't nobody need to mong any more hate;
brotherhood is the real revolution— in Mecca
I was on my knees beside men of every shade.
But how do you get to brotherhood   **here**
where it's so clear that so many people
need their asses kicked.

I already said white skin won't necessarily make someone evil,
though I know what America has done— to white people—
continues to infect them. And they keep draggin their feet
about getting a cure: if it was obvious that I had
something deadly you could *catch*
wouldn't you be, um, *upset,* if I kept saying
Next week I'll see a doctor. Really, I don't feel
all that bad.
                    And anyone who wants to argue
whether or not Europe and her children
have been a blessing or a plague to the rest of us
doesn't really want to argue at all.
Just let them dig through the rubble; let them
do a body count. Ask Africa   Ask India   Ask Asia
Visit a *reservation.*

Look, what I honestly want to talk about
is unity   and how complicated that is, and how
I'm afraid that my life has been a waste, that maybe,
finally, no one will understand what
I'm trying to do. Black Americans
talk about wanting to get even, but don't know
how to take care of each other first.
And I wish I understood what made whites
want to hurt us so much so badly.
Have you ever seen a man lynched? Ever
walked into a ghetto? If you do you'll see
that nothing but dope is keeping a lot of brothers
from chewing off their own hands.

Suppose you were outnumbered and surrounded
by some kind of relentless carnivore
that could come get you anytime, could
snatch you up without even mustering a thought—
and it **is** like that— what would happen
to your mind? Wouldn't you start killing
yourself   rather than waiting to be eaten
alive?
          Black on black crime is
a form of suicide. Gangs, drugs—
they're all part of a community trying
to slit its own wrists. Nobody
wants to deal with this. Sociologists say
build more recreation centers,
Give The Negro More Basketballs,
as if our true home was a gym.

The question is   how do you teach people
who have been taught that they have no value
to love themselves   when even the act of learning
is an act of self-love?

Really, underneath all this talking I do
is just a cry for help from a man close to drowning—
I mean we're all choking on this thing, brother—
America is already underwater.

Sometimes, you're right, sometimes rage
told me what to say, and I meant it   **in my bones**.
But you can't build a bridge out of fire—
I know that now— and you can't take the hand
of a man whose back is to you
                                        and how do you
forgive someone who feels no need to apologize?

I know King worries about this. Jesus
or no Jesus, it **must** drive him crazy sometimes.

You honestly believe Dr. King never dreams
of using his fist?

And you think I *enjoy* being angry?
Nobody was born to be angry.
                              And maybe I
have been foolish. I wanted a place to stand
that would stay beneath my feet. I thought The Nation
of Islam was that place. I believed Elijah Muhammad

had the map, that if I could hold myself steady,
face forward, not blinking, shoes polished and pointed
his way, I would walk right out of this insane,
racist shit right into the truth—

or maybe the truth would find me, the way
a swollen river claims an insect
and carries it to the water's end.
                                        And maybe
that's exactly what happened to me:
once upon a time, I conked my hair, zooted
my suits, smoked reefer   even pimped a little.

Only Allah knows why I didn't die a burglar,
and what it is I've actually become.
And Betty, my wife— I wonder what she sees
when she thinks about *Malcolm X*.
Love? A packed suitcase? A flash
of teeth and glasses as I turn toward the door?

You know what? I'm sick of talking about race—
like I can't have anything else on my mind.

Have you ever seen first dark lie down
across a lake   and what about some nights
some slow jazz sipped straight from the radio?
I want to talk about things worthy of praise—
the fact that somewhere underneath all these colors
we are capable of saying *yes* to each other.

Your newspapers just want a boogie man
to slap on the front page. I want to talk about
what is sacred, how in the Holy Land I pulled
the breath of Allah into my own lungs, how this
made me want to laugh and embrace anyone,
how I want my people to know their skin
unbruised as it had been once
early in the world.

                    But History
is moving on like an old bear
with **all** of us in its belly, and most days,
I sense that it's too late—
my life is shrugging me off,
and there's nothing I can do to explain, to
get it back, nothing I can do to get back
inside it. I get phone calls. I get letters.
People want to kill me: my once beloved
Fruit of Islam   and white people,
maybe FBI.
               For all I know
someone white could pay someone
black to do it   or the reverse.

I'm not so afraid of dying,
but if it were up to me I'd sure try
to live a little while more.
I'd like to live long enough to see
my people sharing books like they do barbecue
or beer— especially the young brothers.

All these big fantasies and hard plans
about spilling my blood— why? What
will change   when I'm gone?   Who's gonna have
such a good time?
                        It's like
I'm on this long street with no intersections.
I'm ready to make a turn, but somebody
keeps taking the corners away—
like in a dream: something bad is after you,
and you're trying to get home,
but your legs are drunk, and you know
it's gaining ground, and when you, just
in the nick of time, touch your door,
it's   *not*   your door   and you know
what's behind you, so somehow you snatch
open your eyes   and, even though
you're sweating in the pitch dark,
you know you're all right, that whatever **it** was,
it can't reach you, not as long as you
stay awake.
                  So, what I wish you'd tell me now
is how I can open my eyes
to get out of *this*.

YOU

are not forgiven
no matter what you say

you are not   you are not   no matter what

The way a man is followed by his shadow, like a three-legged stray,
down all the afternoon streets

so you are followed by our blood
smeared across your teeth

And we are throwing our heads back
dancing still and anyway and almost completely

without you   and your innocence
and your good shoes

No matter when you arrived it was better
before then   Though the words you brought for us
are now inside us

Sometimes I look   and a crowd has gathered   laughing
at someone tied to a tree   and both his arms
are broken   and his clothes are soaked in gasoline

and though it helps
no one now   forgives nothing   now— not at all

I believe it could have been different
I believe you did not think it through

what you were doing   how the others,
those to whom it was done,

might feel about it later
and how difficult   those feelings might be

but maybe *that's tough* as you might say

maybe that's *just too bad*.

III

MARROW

I suppose it is too late to say there is a lesson
in the way a woman's eyes take over an evening,
how her legs move all the tall ships in my blood—

and this thread pulled taut around my belly,
the fluid spool of her hips finding the book of praise
inside me; how old must I get not to feel it

opening like a door in my chest. Inside me
there must be an abandoned city where only
one man lives walking around looking for company,

while inside him someone else calls out
in some other solitary place. To the marrow,
I think this keeps being true.

I have opened my eyes every day for 38 years,
and I am not much wiser, no matter how it all pours in,
but so often and unslowly the world is simply the face

and easy gait of a woman coming into view.
I can't say anything else about it: these open streets
and lamplit avenues; the beautiful names gathering

along the tongue's front edge, a surge of something
like a prayer   for someone to touch, loneliness,
my lungs almost holding on to the air— her mouth
delicious, her legs   one moving next to the other.

PALABRAS

for La Diosa

Here   it is almost ready to rain

It is as if the weather would begin
a long sentence

but keeps stalling over the first few words—

a drop here   three drops   a little wind.

Then, a moment later, the manic stutter of cicadas
who are desperate to explain their thing for trees

but somehow stick on that one odd syllable.
It is this way at times.

A man keeps tapping the tip of his nose,
his brain tensed like a spider,
but what's the use? All sense runs away.

It's as if every word were a roach
and the need to speak
like turning on the kitchen light.

Let's say, for example, that I love you
and must tell you why.

Your eyes . . .   See what I mean?

The taste of your mouth . . .

Do you see how I sweat?

Your fingers. The fields.
The fine, fine weave of your skin.
I want to say so much about so much.

It is as if my heart were crammed with grapes—

each of which I would slip inside you,
then savor lazily lying under a willow
while the long shade wrapped its legs around me.

Of course I talk like this now— my heart
is swollen with grapes

grapes I would steer carefully with my lips
up and over the Aztec-brown swerves *de tus nalgas*

grapes I would squeeze then sip
from the tiny chalice of your navel
while God held both of us in Her all-knowing mouth.

Now everyone wants to question my *appropriateness*.
I can even feel my parents, faraway, squinting
and crossing their arms.

But how can I not say what I'm saying?
Because of you and your witch's walk, woman,

my heart is a grape— big as a man—
a grape full of gasoline, a grape so thoroughly grown

it would be a zeppelin
if it didn't walk around all day
wringing its hands—

a grape that wears glasses, a grape
that breaks chairs, a grape that mumbles
with its mouth full of chips,
a grape so well hidden in itself
that it has disappeared entirely,

and then come these words

all at once, as if from nowhere

like a storm.

FOUR TAKES OF A SIMILAR SITUATION
or
The World Mus Be Retarded

Fine as that Mexican mommy was?
Had me thinkin *jalapeño, hot tamale, arroz*
con pollo an' every other Spanish food
I ever heard about. Hell, I gotta
little bit of a accent just lookin at'er, homebrew.
Yes, indeedy, sweetie, that girl's stuff
was **sho-nuff** meaty. Talkin 'bout
leave that girl alone— is ya crazy?
Even them gay cats be leanin when she bust in!
Had that cinnamon-colored skin
all squeezed into that tight yellow jump-suit
and that smooth-ass salsa-fied strut:
make a brother wanna do them no-hand push-ups, yo—
make you wanna put ya shoes on backward
and run over yourself, make you
mus gotta getta new car, a new pair a'pants
or at leas' a new attitude.

Fine as that sista was?
Wit them tight-ass jeans ripped up jus right—
you know the kind: look like somebody
let Tony The Tiger customize them bad boys
till it was just a cryin shame
how them big choclit thighs come screamin
outta there. Sheee-it! I was so bent over lookin
I coulda tied my shoes wit my teeth— and
she saw that I was seein and she gave me one a'them
uh-huh, yeah looks, like she knew
that I **betta** know she got all the groceries

in one bag. Home-slice, if that honey
had got a holt'a me   it'd been
Humpty-Dumpty all over again—
all the king's horses and all the king's men
woulda jus shook their heads and said, *Yeah, mothafucka,*
*you shoulda **known** you wasn't man enough.*

Fine as that lady was?
Big as China is, they couldn fit
no more fine behind The Great Wall
than Ms. Asia had in her lef earlobe. I won't even
tell you about that thin little light-blue top
she was wearin— **no** bra   **no**where
no how, home-page!
Nipples hard as trigonometry too—
makin that serious jailbreak. Yo,
I gotta cramp in my gums jus from tonguin
the maybe's, baby! And we most certainly do **not**
wanna discuss that black satin sheet a'hair
she had sheenin till a brotha mus gotta
wear shades. And had the nerve to have them rich,
full-bodied Maxwell House lips— damn near
like a sista. Yeah, you can do *The Monkey*
and the *Philly Dog* too, but you can't tell me
that that Chinese chile wasn't sho-nuff bad!
Talkin 'bout who I should and shouldn' be checkin out?
The whole world mus be retarded.

Fine as Ms. white girl was?
Fuck all y'all crazy mothafuckas!
I don know if she was prejudice or not

but the honey had them big, strong-ass
white girl calves— and one a'them slit skirts
that talk to ya when she walk—
and backed it up witta little bit a'bootie:
I'm tellin you dead-up, yo— I was ready
to forgive the sins of her fathers right then and **there**!
Had that kinda curly, halfway frizzy red-brown hair,
she coulda been Jewish, Scottish, Octoroon, Italian—
only her hairdresser knows, hometown, but
if the honey had said, *looka'here, mista,*
I think I wanna waltz— brotha, you betta know
I had my dancin shoes wit me.

RUSH

Let's slow it   all down
so the sparrows   sound like bullfrogs
and the bullfrogs   low like cattle
and the cows   become four-legged tubas
and the tubas   play the music
redwoods make   when they groove
long roots   into earth

And this afternoon   around 4 o'clock
the second-hand   will be   almost asleep
the tick   so far   from the tock
they could be   two whales   in two separate seas
and when you come   at that hour
with someone's mouth   like sangria

it will last   for weeks   one
slow gasp   after another   after
the next   your heart   like the lazy giant
chasing Jack   stealing the goose
with the golden eggs   Fe
Fi
        Fo

VALENTINE'S DAY

for Tony Hoagland

I saw an X-rated movie once
where a man, a minor clerk—
faced with having to watch
his boss push himself
between the rippling thighs
of an athletic secretary—
went moping behind a file cabinet,
unzipped his blue corduroys
and began to give himself
head.   Really.   It was
not a camera trick.

I was appalled, of course,
not only because of the size
of that turgid jam-hamster, but
because here was a man exercising
an option I'd never even considered—
a true do-it-yourselfer, a renegade
in the world of wanting, a man
who could have his cake and well,
you know.

Think about this guy growing up,
going to high school, believing English
was just okay, strolling to the showers
with a cool smirk. It must have been
quite a day when he first leaned over
and kept going down. That dumb joke
about how hard it is to kiss your own elbow
must've seemed pretty goddamn dumb.

Maybe he was fifteen, maybe it was Sunday—
a rainy, after-church afternoon
when the big itch he felt
for Delores, the math whiz, sent him
back upstairs to his room
to check the little voice he heard
tiptoeing from his pants, so he
unzipped and stretched his neck
to listen, then found himself
able to kiss the taut, ready skin.
And maybe this was the beginning

of an adjustment, a maneuver,
unique unto him— just one hard turn
away from all the booby traps
and regulations set up to keep us
from the thousand variations
of hands, of lips, of genitalia,
of all the things they can do.
Who hasn't dreamed of being
fucked perfectly— once
and for all— if only
on Valentine's Day?

Who hasn't craved a fine stranger
walking past, sliding like a
tropical mist along the coast of you,
or something a wee bit wilder—
the game of 3   in a loose knot.
Once, I got a phone call
from a guy who called himself
the banana man,
asking if I would let him
blow me.

And after awhile you have to wonder
just how lonely someone might be
in America, this country where
actual adults get on TV and tell *Oprah*,
"if we didn't bring it up so much
maybe young people wouldn't get
involved in sex"— as if sex
were a sort of larceny, this place
where a man can get on talk-radio
stuttering, "AIDS will m-ma-make us
m-moral again." And I think by now

everybody should feel just a little
more sorry for everyone else—
each of us being the exact thing
some others of us want, but
usually cannot have, for whichever
reason: fear, guilt, bad attitude,
shyness, simple fatigue.

So we end up at the movies
or deep in magazines or alone,
teasing our own skin   or just
wishing,

just wishing we could slam the door
on the whole thing and just be inside
on the phone, happy, talking
to our happy friends about
nothing at all and how easy it is
to come by.

SUMMER

for M

Say there is a bridge,

and sunlight
like a trillion tiny stars

on the water beneath,

and say the afternoon
is the sound of heat

standing in the trees.

Maybe someone could know
about love

at such an hour— summer
offering itself

like an absence, like something almost nearby.

The future turning over
its open empty hands.

The tapered stretch of her white back.

No breeze.
A clumsy blue insect bending a leaf.

Her hair. The way it smelled sometimes.

LIFE ACCORDING TO REGGIE

When my mother squeezed me
out of her body like a knotty seed
from the sweet flesh of a peach,
and Dr. Billicks slapped me— twice—
on my brand new baby's behind,
I had a pretty good idea
that an attitude problem had
gotten loose in the world, that if
something was *rotten in Denmark*,
some shit had gone wrong here too,
that no place I was going
would ever be nice
as where I'd been   kicking around
to the murmuring stadium noise
of my mother's lungs and heart.

I had one of those
sneaking suspicions, dangling
by my feet there   in the well-known
sawed-off light of reality,
that whatever was real would be
different from what I'd spend my days
dreaming about,
that there'd be times when
just lifting my head off my chest,
just not bursting
into tears, would be
a trophy to be proud about.

You guys know what I mean—
you see people running around out here

clearly dazed by the constant smack
of what goes on,
like those over-matched boxers
who try to grin and look confident
when they know they can't
take another punch
without falling down.

If only I had known
that there would be a willingness
to do what they did
to Kennedy's head, that
there would be "death squads"
in El Salvador, that I could
inherit a country
so messed up about race—

if, as a bouncy bubbly, I had had
a way to figure that there
might, in fact, be a
Pope   in the world
I would have been born,
blown my mom a kiss,
and squeezed right back in.

But as it stands, I'm out here
with everybody else, wondering what
to wonder, having damn near forgotten
where it all began. You guys
know what I mean.
You see how it is.

LATIN

Words slip into a language the way
white-green vines slide between slats in a fence.

A couple opens the door to a restaurant,
sees the orange and black colors everywhere

and the waitress grins, "Yeah,
a little Halloween overkill, huh."

Overkill, a noun for all of us
fidgeting under the nuclear umbrella—

but for that instant it just meant too many decorations,
too many paper skeletons and hobgobbled balloons.

———————

I know a woman who is tall with dark hair,
who makes me think of honeysuckle

whenever she opens her legs. Not just the flower
but the dew-soaked music itself   *honeysuckle*   like a flavor.

And I remember the first time years back
when LaTina told me what it was we had

between our eight-year-old front teeth
that April afternoon, our hands wet

with rain from the vines. "Honey sickle," she said,
while the white flower bloomed from the side of her mouth,

and I had a new sweetness on my tongue and a word
I'd never heard before. How was it decided in the beginning?

This word   for *this* particular thing,
a sound attached to a shape or a feeling forever.

All summer long the cicadas don't know
what we call them.

They sneak from the ground every year after dark,
break out of their shells right into the language,

and it holds them like a net made of nothing
but the need to make strange things familiar.

All summer long they rattle trees like maracas
until they become part of our weather—

quiet in rain, crazy in hard sun,
so we say *those cicadas sure make enough noise, huh.*

And the noise of that sentence   heard ten-thousand times
becomes a name for *us* the cicadas keep trying to say.

I think about dying sometimes,
not the sudden death in the movies—

the red hole in the shirt, the eyes
open like magazines left on a waiting room table—

not that, but withering slowly like a language,
barely holding on until everything

I ever did or said   is just gone, absorbed
into something I would never have imagined—

like Latin. Not lost completely, but moved away
from that bright, small place

between seeing   and naming,
between the slow roll of ocean

and the quick intake of air
that would fill the word *wave*.

CULTURE

for Tracy Chapman

Like a wave

When they came they came

like a wave

Not like a wave from the sea
Not like the wave a boat makes cutting water

but like a wave

When they came
they came

and it looked like a big wave
carried them

the way a big wind carries columns of rain

or maybe the wave was them
rolling as a wave would roll

Not a wave of sorrow
like those that rush the heart
Not a wave of confusion

Not a wave of heat
like one that comes in summer

More like a wave

than a wave

When they
came they came

as you might imagine a wave hurrying
to come ashore

Not like a wave of sound
though they were heard
Not like the wave of a hand
though we did greet them

when they came they
just kept coming

until we couldn't see
across them   until we couldn't
see around them until

looking at them was like looking
at the ocean from an island

and the wave
carried some of us
like a wave

as though in a way we'd
become a part of it
this motion   this constant shove

as though being the wave
meant we couldn't do anything
about the wave   but be it

the way water in the surf can't fight
the walking of the tides

But this wave they came in
wasn't a wave exactly

but it seemed to seem
like a wave would seem if
one had come

There was something inevitable about it
the way it came as they came

the way it carried some of us along
for awhile   for a pretty long while

as though it were our destiny
not like a wave would
carry something   but like a wave

would   carry something
unlike a wave

like a wave

MANIC

A Conversation With Jimi Hendrix

Berkeley, CA   August 1970

All these hang-ups, all this time wasted when
everything really could be really groovy. I mean
I'm not tryin to come down on anybody, you know,
but the whole thing is a big, fat comedown—
nobody think I notice that almost all my audience
is mostly white. Man, I'm not blind and I can't   I mean
music isn't about whether your skin   how your skin is.
Music is somebody arguing with God. It's about
what you feel about bein alive,
here, right now: Vietnam to the left of you—
Watts to the right   and straight ahead, the future
like a really beautiful girl whose face you can't
quite make out— maybe 'cause you're scared, maybe
'cause you're so busy pretending, so wrapped up
in cellophane   you forget to unzip your heart.

We can't go on livin like this, and anyway, you can tell
the world is begging for a change— where you're loved
for who you are   instead of for what you got from Sears
and whoever. Ever since the beginning of America
they been sellin us this idea that buying things
make you a better person, but it just make you a slave—
them things you got **got you**   as much as you got them.
You're workin every day without a minute to make love in,
tryin to pay for all your pretty wall-to-wall rugs
and fur this and leather that, knowin all the time
your life is zoomin by in one a'them *wish-I-had-a* cadillacs.

And all this bad electricity between the races—
I think alotta people, well everybody, everybody,
well   almost everybody is tired'a bein afraid
and then actin like their fear is really hate
and then hurting people which just causes more fear
and hate and on and on down the yellow brick road
to where you can't even say hello to a body
unless they're your mother and lord knows
you better not **love** nobody of another shade.

I mean, what kind of life is that— *I would love you,*
but you're too dark, you're too light, you're
too beige? I mean, here were are, all of us, ridin
on the back of this huge, iridescent dragonfly
called Earth   And all we can think, the best we can do
is keep comin up with new ways to make it impossible
to live together. Even the devil gotta be amazed
at how we're tearin ourselves apart— more in love
with money than with people. So sad, so sad.

But at the same time alotta people are lazy.
All they wanna do is be angry.
They don't try to **become** something new—
which is the only way the world ever really changes.
If we keep runnin around with all these sledgehammers,
and all the governments do is send in more pigs,
man, it's just gonna be a big mess.
And music has got to help. Definitely.
The music has got to become a new religion.
All these *thou-shalts* and *you-better-nots*
hasn't gotten us no closer to heaven. Matter a'fact,

it's just the opposite: 90% of the people act afraid
of their bodies, scared to be naked. That
doesn't seem helpful, not at all.

Our bodies are a hundred percent natural.
You don't see nobody puttin boxer shorts on zebras.
But that's all part of the pretense: if you keep
your pin-stripe suit on you can play like
you're not part of the jungle. Without your body
you're not here.   Like God ain't got nothin
better to do than be bashful. Like the Pope
all buried in curtains: we don't need him. What kind
of example is that? The music has got to teach
that **anybody** can be Jesus— woman or man— but
that's like the *M&M* candy thing, you know,
melts in your mouth, not in your hand: talkin
is not enough. You gotta push.

I wanna play for everybody— Cleopatra, people in
Nigeria— wouldn' mind jammin behind the Great Wall,
but I still don't consider myself *ambitious*.
Seem like such a military term   and we don't need
no more soldiers. We need to cut down on dyin.
Once upon a time I was s'posed to be a paratrooper.
I was in the army and everything, but I got hurt
on a practice jump. Some leprechaun reached up,
twisted my ankle and saved my behind.
When they get you in a uniform you become capable
of some very scary things, man— like who was born
to *take orders*? Who jumps out of a plane
just to land in a scene where people want to shoot you?

Don't get me wrong: we're all just babies down here—
even soldiers   but somebody flips you into *your country*,
some goat-eyed general draws some lines on a map,
next thing you know you're in *their country*,
in their jungle, lickin somebody's blood
off your bayonet. But I try to stay positive,
play loud like a baby cryin for his mama. But damn,
even at Woodstock you're not sure they can hear you,
like maybe nobody can dig why you're up there
fussin with the strings, searchin for those notes
that make you more than entertainment. Sammy Davis
is cool   so's Frank Sinatra, but a guitar solo
can be a sermon— know what I mean?

Most of the time I just can't do it
and I get so mad, but some days, like
at Rainbow Bridge, everything comes: the beach
right behind the stage, the blue-green sea,
gallons of grape wine and grass, no tickets, no
pigs, no buttons to push, and we made a music that day
that made at least one angel glad— there was this breeze
like ostriches   like ostrich feathers
being drug over you again and again—
now who do you think was behind that?

And all that day, man, nobody died. You might think
I'm losin my mind, but I had this feeling all day
that **nobody** in the whole world died— ol'man Death
was spendin the weekend in some other Milky Way.
And that's how it should be. I mean, I believe music
can save people   because most a'the time people

die too easy, like they're already halfway gone
and any little nudge sends'em right to the next world.
Good music can remind you why it's, why livin,
what livin is, you know— well, I guess if you watch
"The Wild Kingdom" sometimes, after'while
you might have your doubts, but when I go,

they gonna have to pry me loose from here,
dig me out witta steam shovel— at least,
that's the way I feel about it now. Later on,
I might get really tired of all this and just
drift downstream   or I could just disappear, zap!
like some bug snatched by a bullfrog.
Or I might take it to another level, slip into
Sherwood Forest   turn into a Cheshire Cat—
you know   a *Hendrix In Wonderland* type a'thing,
which could be really outtasight when you think about it,
you know   just a smile— all that's left of you
is a smile, you know.

IV

RECOGNIZED

for Newt Gingrich

Sun up.
There they are.

The low clouds
like a herd of gray horses

running north over the trees.

Daylight and his insects flex their teeth.

Trafficking the green field
a small city of crows.

Each cawing *mine!   mine!*

Something we know
better than

is being seconded. The blessed nod
to the privileged.

Underneath the scab our mouths have
healed closed.

The Congress of Shrunken Heads and Dumb Clucks
has declared the season
open.

And the pale animals don't mind it's okay.
Almost nothing has ever broken
their skin.

Bright. Bright.

You can see fresh commercials
starring in their eyes.

Like a dumb question   like a free bird

Help comes looking for a
few suggestions.

Help comes ready to be recognized, but

KEROSENE

after the L.A. riot,
April 1992*

In my country   the weather
it's not too good   At every bus stop anger
holds her umbrella folded her
face buckled tight as a boot   Along the avenues
beneath parked cars spent
cartridges glimmer   A man's head crushed
by nightsticks   smoke still
slides from his mouth   Let out wearing

uniforms   hyenas rove in packs
unmuzzled and brothers strain inside
their brown skins   like something wounded
thrown into a lake   Slowly
like blood filling
cracks in the street slowly   the
President   arrived   his mouth
slit into his face   Like candles seen
through thick curtains   sometimes
at night   the dark citizens
occur to him

like fishing lamps along
the black shore of a lake   like moths
soaked in kerosene   and lit

*George Bush was still in office at this time.

GOOD HAIR

for Derrick Bell

Like anybody, I would like to live   a long life.
Longevity   has its place.

Much of this is already decided.

And there must be good reasons, I guess.

But if everybody died tomorrow   what
would the point have been?

Power? The strength to do unto others   and not get done unto?

If I can hit you and not get hit back   I can change
your life.

Mmmmm. Nutritious Rodney King.

I lived in the time of the whites.
Europe and America ran the globe.

Like two related sets of big, sharp, smiley teeth.

   "But my family never had slaves."

———————

Let us not seek to satisfy our thirst for freedom
by drinking from the cup of bitterness and hatred.

A lot of this seems settled.
Capitalism makes everything glisten.

"Come to Jamaica. Come back to the way things used to be."

For who?

I lived in the time of power. Whites?
They had an angle. They had the edge.

They wrote it down. They worked it out.

But for us   there were sports. There was **basketball**.

---

*It came as a joyous daybreak   to end the long night
of their captivity.*

It seemed like everything we did was a reaction to them.

The music we made. The way we talked.

We started "good hair" and "bad hair." And blues.
And "high-yellow"   and "too dark."

My parents spent their lives proving they were
    "as good as   if not better than."

    "Guess Who's Coming to Dinner?"

I give up. Tell me.

Who **was**   Sidney Poitier   in that movie?

When all of god's children— black men and white men, jews and gentiles,
protestants and catholics— will be able to join hands and sing
in the words of the old Negro spiritual . . .

What made Sammy Davis   kiss Richard Nixon?
Who made Step'n' Fetchit?

Power is the capacity to turn others' lives to your advantage.

In Ethiopia and Guatemala not many
get rich helping others lose weight.

    "With a bullwhip and a little time on your hands
     you can slice a nigger into beef jerky," he grinned.

———————————

So History rises up on hind legs and starts
sniffing for something to eat.

Something like profit. Something like you. Something like
Michael Jordan.   "Be like Mike."

While I lived, I was never exactly sure where I was
bleeding from.

    "Mr. Seibles, where I come from black men   are **black**.
     In Gambia we would see your light-brown skin, and we would
     not say brother."

The marvelous new militancy   which has engulfed the Negro Community
must not lead us to distrust of all white people . . .

And now, it is done. The house no one meant
to build. But

look at it— perfect— even the trim.
Where else could you live?

———————————

Evil has grown so stylish   and beautiful.

So young and restless.

  "How come none of the white countries
    get to be part of the Third World?"

Power? How do you ignore power?

*I've seen   the Promised Land. I may not get there with you,
but I want you to know **tonight**, that we, as a people,
will get to the Promised Land!*

Sometimes I think my head is going to explode.

Mmmmm. Nutritious Rush Limbaugh.

Imagine someone biting into your face over and over,
but you have to keep acting like nothing's wrong.

Imagine someone saying, "But my family never had slaves."

A lot of days like this.

I lived in the time   when the capacity to kill
and take from others

and feed your fat fuckin' face   and not remember
was power.

Times when I think I've just landed from some other world.

Like I don't really speak the language,
but people nod and play along.

What did it mean, does it mean? Being white.

I lived in America. It was never quite explained.

Note: All italicized text came from the various speeches
        made by Dr. Martin Luther King, Jr.

NO MONEY DOWN, TAKE IT HOME TODAY: IT'S *YOURS*

Sun climbs over the trees
and light runs toward you,

runs flailing its fast golden legs
like a good dog who's been lost for years—

now seen again   there   in the park—
who turns around before you can even whistle a name,

as though just the one wish in your eyes
were loud enough to bring it all back,

the big, shaggy ball of sun blazing like a happy collie
back into your life, licking your face, asking

*Where have you **been**?*
Where, oh where have you been?

MIDNIGHT: THE COYOTE, DOWN IN THE MOUTH

I used to sleep so well
my mother could carry me
by the neck scruff without
waking me up. Even the dark
tasted good with the quiet noise
of family around me— and sunrise
simply meant I could catch
grasshoppers drunk on dew.
Of course, I didn't know
the road-runner then,
and whatever I wanted
seemed nearby and easy.

Now, I close my eyes
and he's there   in slow-motion
technicolor, all a'trot,
his heart like a little
tom-tom, loud enough to be
visible inside that
boney chest. Come morning
it'll be the same, but hotter—
a buzz of shins, the road
sizzling like a fuse.
Meep.   Meep.

I used to believe what I did
mattered in some spectacular way,
as if a big audience sat somewhere
really watching, really
wondering how well I would do

out here. At first, I
thought it was only a matter
of time. I'd put on a bib,
pick up some silverware, duck
behind a cactus— just to
ham it up a little.
He was mine: I figured
a few near-misses for sus-
pense   then *chomp!* The
good life. Of course.

I've been after the road-runner
for so long— I can't tell
if it's hunger, love, or
just plain stupidity.
Maybe that's what's so
goddamn funny: my life
whittled down to a riot
of wild pursuits and slim
chances to grab something I
don't even understand. I mean,
if I had his speed I'd get
the hell away from here. I'd
be so gone even color
couldn't catch me.

It's crazy. I've died
lots of times. Lots. Blown-up.
Bowled over by boulders.
Run over by trucks.

Some days, when I'm a 1000 feet
below the ledge and a
1000 more from impact, I stop
and look up at that
pebble-headed feather-duster
and touch my chin. Who
keeps bringing me back? How
can I keep hitting the ground
and getting up with nothing
but another perfect scheme?

It's got to end somewhere,
doesn't it? There's got to be
some way to   I don't even
wanna **be** a coyote anymore,
canniverist-sharpist-toothist.
It's not me— it's like my
appetite doesn't belong
in my belly, like I'm hungry
because   someone else wants
to eat, like I'm stuck in this story
no matter how bad I want
to get out— and me trying
to get out of the story
IS the story. Nevermind.

Of course, I think my life
means something.
And, of course, it does.
Otherwise, I'd be running around
all the time and there'd be

no— it would seem like
my life had been,
I mean, who hasn't wondered,
right? But if this
is not my life, then
what am I doing?
And who should I ask?

Honestly, if you can just
stand still for a minute you

start to see the whole
show. I mean— it's all

perspective; if you can
step out of the action

long enough to catch
your breath you

become your **own**
audience. And, of course,

there you are,
a scrawny animal
starving in the middle

of a desert,
squeezing your knife
and fork.

VOCABULARY BROTHER: THE EDITORIAL

after Daman Wayans
from "In Living Color"

Unless I am suddenly uninformed of concurrent hypotheses,
I feel that it is compulsive of me to regurgitate irrationally
regarding the matter at hand. In these coitally disruptive times
it often seems that an erect man must step forward and remain
rigid, erstwhile others merely arouse themselves
in the poignancy of their own homes. My primary point
is quite impertinent: however hazardous
the recent fellatio of the community may appear,
there can be little doubt that all of us, black as well as white,
wish to be blown completely out of proportion.

In a parallel manner, I think it must be lionized
that inasmuch as each of us is intangible,
his or her intestinal ambition remains a source
of fragrant advertisement which, in turn, promotes the combustion
of what can only be regarded as the inescapable tampax
of contemporary society— which is certainly not to plug
the seminal point of view that, in the proper uterus,
might deserve a wide speculum of hasty investigations.

Nonetheless, the Clinton Administration's approach to these vexations
could be comparably compared to what heretofore, ipso facto
corroborates the untold alibi of unanesthetized vasectomy.
And finally, I would just like to conclude that
without some dedicated probing into the irrigated womb
or our urban predicament, you and I could be left in dire need
of lubrication, brimming with future ejaculations
in an America frothing with cultural richness.

Thank you.

HEY

To God's hairy ears, all this sad jibber-
jabber sounds like a bad baby peeing
on a plastic hymnal. Turn out
that serious face. Put down
your poison. In between everything
between us, everything keeps keeping
a cookbook of possible kisses, delicious
circumstance. It is only by being stupid
that we follow the scared into the lonely.

Listen. Enough money for the church.
Enough dog days. The bank & business boys
cannot stop this mutiny, this late allegiance
to the whispering in the blood. Why
let anybody starve? Why is it
so hard to be happy? Shhh.
You already know
what the blood is saying.

Tonight. I am a shadow. With one hand
made of light. This is the beginning
of a new weather— this shared breath, this
open secret. Hey, look how large
the wind is   and still you do not see it.
Ghosts of all good kinds have gathered
to shake the *hully-gully*
in your thighs. Surrey on down.
Hurry. There is already something
in just your size.

WHAT YOU REALLY WANT:

To seem normal. To believe normal.
To feel full of normalness. And not to worry

secretly that someone might read your
I'm-okay face like a toupee.

And pluck it off. And point to the door.

To walk among Americans. Just like
one of the gang. A chum among chums.

Cool wit' the cool wit' the cool.

To see a church and not. Feel like throwing
up. To believe that something holy. **Is** in there.

To have your cup filled to the brim. With
delicious normality. Mmmmmmm.

And applaud the year's new cars from Chevrolet.
Yeah-heah-heah!

To not mind being a member. Of a country utterly
shaped by money hunger— a money chase   a money party.

Pin the tail on the money.

And manliness. The quest for the firmest. Handshake of all.

And race. To tra-la-la through the wide rivers
of whites. Unnoticed and not noticing your unnoticedness.

And move among the brothers. Without eyes of steel.
Without arms like nails.

To feel a singular history propping you up.

Instead of having. Each part of your face. Questioning the other.

And not dying. To not be dying of something. Not
thinking. About not dying.

But not realizing it.
To spend living like a kind of forever. Being

insanely relaxed. Fearless— a puppy wagging up to everybody.
We're friends! We're friends!

THE GUST

In the mind
there comes a moment
when shadows fall back   like men
from a gust of something,
when the brain is light
as a fly on your wrist

and in the jeweled eyes of that fly
you see your own six-legged self
white-shoed, dancing,
swinging on parade—

the gold tuba grown from your lips:
Zoom pah dah cha-cha
Zoom pah dah cha-cha
Zoom pah dahhh

TEN MILES AN HOUR

The weird thing about the place was the speed of light—
8, 9 miles an hour, tops. I sweartagod!
It was beautiful though, the way it felt slowing over you
like a balmy breeze— light slow enough to catch in a,
in a cup, light you could smear on a slice of bread
like jam, light you could rub into your hair like *Sulfur 8*.

And there were other things. For example,
just about everybody but little kids could outrun it,
something we never consider here with the photons
clockin' 186,000 miles a second. So, say you saw
some skinhead mothafucka with a swastika on his cheek.
You could holler, *Hey, you piss-brain, duck-steppin,
kitty-litter suckin, sick-ass Nazi*, then take off.
Once you hit 10 mph you would disappear
till you broke back to a trot. That's the beauty
of slow light— no muss, no fuss:
now you see a brother   now you don't.

Anyway, this is how it really went. First,
I should say there were no cars for obvious reasons,
and getting to this spot is a long haul on foot:
down this long alley, over three rocky hills,
gotta wade through this one muddy river,
and there's a forest somewhere, dark and spooky—
made me feel like Red Riding Hood.
So, when I arrive I'm tired and my sneaks are soggy,
like I'm wearing wet biscuits on my feet. Everything
looks blurry— like, like when you move a camera
just as you snap the shot.

Pretty soon though, I notice nobody's poor   nobody,
and I come to this park and there's a sister
straddling this Hawaiian dude who's sitting on a bench.
Her skirt's hiked up, she got them big legs shinin',
and I mean they're gettin' it, gettin' it good
to the last drop right there. And it wasn't about
showin' off. They could'a been hid way away somewhere,
two good people takin' care of business, you know—
T-C'in' on the B like it wasn't no helluva big thing.

And there was this bunch of reddish-gold birds—
looked like pigeons— and all these kinky-haired kids
chasing them across the grass with painted leaves,
and together they made a noise like someone   someone
munching CrackerJacks near a microphone.

So, I just start dancin'— no music but that— I just
take off my clothes and start wavin' my arms and hoppin'.
I'm steady shakin' my yams, my jammy's jingle-jumpin',
and pretty soon it's me and two other brothers   then,
these Turkish cats fall in on congas   and this
Jewish honey and her extremely fine friend from Laos—
I sweartagod! And **then**   this Ethiopian mamasita, a real
killer-diller, busts in the circle wit' this Mexican,
Mississippi-Masala-lookin' girl, and I turn
to this Eastern Bloc brother named Gustav and holla'
Oh no, say it ain't so— don' NObody need to have
no BODY like that! So, we grab our gear, get dressed,
and follow them to this place called *Logan's*: black tables,
big sofas, soft single chairs covered in lazuli blue.

Somebody hits the dimmers. I ride the light over slow, like,
like a loose clump of new weather, and open my mouth
to the first words that gang-up inside my teeth, *Excuse me,*
ladies, but my blood's all tied in a knot, and I
was wondering if you might help me get it undone.
Ethiopia nudges Mexico and asks me if the knot in question
might require *both* of them. No lie!
But I don't wanna fade on Gustav; I nod his way. Like smoke,
his smile floats over. So, she closes her eyes and I see
that her friend's hand has wandered under her dress,
lingering there with small, graceful undulations. I'm
diggin' it, but I'm not sure what it means. So,
I shrug and get ready to step back when Mexico says
Taste this, holding up two wet fingers.

Well, what would you have done? Been scared
and said, *Um, no thanks— I'm driving.* Man,
I could spend my life tryin' to name that flavor.
Anyway, Alandra (that's her name), gets up with them legs
that go   *all*   the way down, and I can feel some story
starting to untell, my body calling *open-says-a-me*
to all its magic doors. Next thing I know,
we're dancing to this oldie slow jam:

> *I'm an ever-rolling wheel*
> *without a destination real*
> *I'm an ever-spinning top*
> *going around   till I drop*

You know that moment when two bodies find out
how they fit together, as though one torso

is hinged to the other, as though you're both
perfectly matched pieces in some sweet, nobody-ever-
told-you-about-it, sho-nuff forever and always jigsaw—
me and Alandra are falling into place.

You got me going in circles

         Later, we step outside. It's sundown.
You could see the last puddles of sunlight
drying up, going dark, and the streetlamps
slowly throwing their lazy glow like Rapunzel
rolling down her three stories of hair.

I mean, up until just now, I thought I might still have been
standing somewhere in America, but the night held no threat,
and across the road, I remember, two men resting in each other's arms.

And her kiss, the taste of her mouth opening like a sleepy carnival
into mine, and Gustav and Genet against the magnolia, fucking
like dancing, like doing some delicious naked salsa,

my lungs squeezing more and more oxygen into my blood, my brain
bright orange like a tropical fish, Alandra bringing me
into her skin, holding on, taking me up like some kind of
origami bird she could balance on her lips.

And the *not-out* moon, the sharp whelming of what
is never seen   and the voice coming all undone,
but for the one long syllable, and I sweartagod!

112

There is a place not all that far from here
where glad drums whistle
all the answers to the riddles of bone.

Say whatchuwanna, but inside my hand
there is a sound, and inside that sound
there is a city, and inside that city
it is early— with you already awake,

your hand like mine, like a rooster,
throwing itself open, loud, each finger
a street vendor crowing the first light
free— along with all the big, blue-apple muffins,
the crowded carts of cantalope, and the T-shirts

and the clear castle of air,
and everything else   everything